A Drawn Confirmity

In
Verse

Rick Bryan

A Drawn Confirmity

In

Verse

*Special thanks to Bruce Bartman
for analysis of protocols.*

CONTENTS

A DRAWN CONFIRMITY

A drawn confirmity
Dimmed as such intent in white
May have woven of surface
Nets drape undertow currents
Underveined pulsated arterial
Red of sea sketch
From a furtherance

The tips of her fingers
Semblance and ladies their hair
Adorned figurative
Sudden hats simply in pixel
Incandescent in finery brushed
Spangled of oil on canvas
So as they are

Splendor her looking back
Awaiting atide of waves
The time of waves
Of sequent the sea risen
In Carthage gale of Calais
Then of yellows impressioned
So as she was.

Soundscape: Silent Dream / Lemongrass

ALL THE SIGHT OF

*All the sight of
At the good moment
About then I've seen
Unlikely there was
As there had been other though
All in a flash
Played out such as*

*Noisily thrush the birds
Later they are back again
And the prettiest girl standing there
Stepped into image
Plain as velvet
Were I was as ought
A word to say*

*Of a modern world
Come down the furtherence
A laugh and high ceilinged skies
Like that blinked
Or never mentioned
At the time
Slanting between us
Of the fuss about and smile.*

Soundscape: Wise One / John Coltrane Quartet

AS OF IN WATER

As of in water heroine of fathom
Turn bloom a silver hand
And wrote a first letter
So on steadily her very name
Earth and season
Shone back one after another
And put on my best
And that is that

Of a blind love kind
Heard not first form
Was nothing to do with it
Anything to go by of
Even so it keeps on
What so ever a mindset
By then at all upon my intent
The thing of it is

Nothing I should to do
A count on my fingers
Ring and ring just that
Of a kind supposed
Talking to her on the phone
By mid light and that
As it would be

Soundscape: Out of this World / John Coltrane

So well in the keeping of
As you've said
In mid set at the least
And there you have it
A bit of jabbing
Front me up as it was

Such the adrafting form
Unfolded of coming to
Completions and discretion
Drop and by drop
As of in water
Shut me by evening fire
That which is the last of
In morning silence the room
Brightens.

BREATH OF AIR

Breath of air I nerve myself
To say of it a worth while
She had an idea of it
Fresh white blossoms she could bare
Something alike the silenced change
To a shadow eyes thrown
As daylight falls
What I couldn't say
And then whatsoever
Abstracted light by degree

Back felled just the same
Having a word of it
And opaque as this
The birds an indifference
Here dashed of clouds
Informal aside indistinct
Of other things

Soundscape: Ile Tropicale / Oasis de Detente et Relaxation

Or in kind a play between
Entangled enflamed seamed against
Simply all that comes to mind
Down to the considering
Of darker points of days
All that has been taken in

My eyes drawn away
Vague bell chimes of a sort
Were you there on the brink
A time ago in your eyes
Of an afternoon a phrase
A differing gauge
The sensed as well indiffering
No definite plans of a day
What as such and what the better
And so on and so on.

DRAPINGS

Drapings entangle the floor
A sensitivity of aspect
At some turn the last stretch
Linking of voices as far a distance
Then up the last step a scarf off her head
A dismissive laugh remembered
Water rims the partial out point
So to impression the lightening of

And got my breath perhaps or pointlessly
Said but an aside
A day in all well the rain came
Among shadows held in presence
Consuming skies so closer
To refract in blue stay
On the thinking of what no doubt
Of these days the whole story

Soundscape: Ile Tropicale / Oasis de Detante et Relaxation

The enchantment of the matter
Newly hedged brooks the water
Drawing of as to walk as unheard
And all over the whitening of moons
Meteor showers landing of trees
That of would have imaged best belief
One after another keeping an eye in the way of
Water funneled continuance
Things the while unloosed extravagance
A bit of spree in the density scape.

HOW TELL

How tell begins out
To bare than other it is
Nothingly accorded less
Turns as forgotten of which
What comes to mind
Begins chaptered fervent
Of quite modern time referring

A house on a crowding hill
A coastal flat
Stepped into blue of which
Setting of water
Nearing a defined edge

And lightly into water as it is
As it is the wishing of it
A walk out in the coolness
Settling of water
Seeing of rustic
In vapor such as intends
Over me.

Soundscape: AirplaneShadows / Kiln

IN THE LIGHT OF

In the light of the clear
So do I
Duplexity of gesture
Its own mark
How peered from the window
Do tell
An entourage and the entering of pantheon
Therefore newfold
That you can see it very well
As a star book of
Quiet of every tree in the wind

Will you will you merely
Flame and pulse of the crux
It must quite
Such the way does one's heart
Then such one day was such
Or so to my surprise
Play it as it is
The good ear pending
This is the lift of it
The blackout the airlock
The faint trapeze
Appearing outline of.

Soundscape: Ile Tropicale / Oasis de Detente et Relaxation

IN THE MIDDLE

In the middle of the precise and more likely
Certainly of but only the reason for
For I've often pictured it
As over their hearts on nearby hills
Songs seemingly so to notice
So to refer

How is it that one would but forever
And then to live forever
The when of this having done so
Going on one of two ways
Sketch anything you want
That remains

Trying to decide
Starting over from everything
A piece goes missing a piece of fact
Looking then and now would you breath
And then we're almost settled in turn
I lay on the grass
Leaned as such on the image

Soundscape: Silent Dream / Lemongrass

Under level the shore recedes
That one had dreamed
Draped in the downing of rest
Of wind whereupon is heard
Shadowed that you were
Birds in the trees what shall we do
And the life long day
Beyond and some certainty.

IN THE NIGHTINGALE

In the nightingale
Moonlight perches
Along the aqualine
The waters of the bay
Stars I see
They are seen
Thrown then in the air
Ornament observing

Leaves and roots to bury
At the monolith
Here was that of which
It's like
Tell you what it's like
But you've got it
Being the business of getting it right
A set of pasteboard cards
And elaborating this
Sparkling to the maxim
What you find

Soundscape: Cootes Paradise / Danna & Clement

Cast on the water
Incline with rather downcast eyes
Of seaweedy rocks
A voice wished into as though
Everyone to their taste
Take it for granted
Everyone thought the world of
In sterling good and beautiful eyes.

IN THE NOOK

In the nook where I lie
Were immense vistas appeared
Onto roofs out over as occur
Straight pieces an up set lined within
First rendered in glint hopeful
Perilous would you dare
From the start felt to be turned to
To mention vast shines of
Taken note as to heart

Blue and ocher of these musts to do
And otherwise
To end a tale streaked with
Particulars and starlight of
Water hyacinth of myriad
On reefs rather away the clearing
The pardon I would
Running out drizzling out
Far of the air at hour's end

Soundscape: No Plan / David Bowie

Saga here we go
Slipped their names at ease
Thinking of the last of
In a world someone passing in the street
Said and I'd looked around
Generally agreeing smack in the middle

In the cold year as
And any excuse then
And that was as the way it was
So do they run she wrote
Rushed across the bridge
Wrought iron grating
Very finely felled back
In coasting of a blade like
Streamed edges of running luck.

IN YOUR EYES

In your eyes
There of our tears
Unwinds extroadinarily
Your mother's picture
Holding absolute
Decisioned so of then
Into eternity stepped
Goodbye all at once

Holding back endless
One two three counts
Of everything
Thereout light breaks
For what intent lingers the sky
Arc angel above
That readily sure
A movement of your hand.

Soundscape: Freesia / Kevin Kendle

METHODICAL

Methodical and taken to account
Thinking the topography of air the air torn
A point on the hour full tilt a look back
The actual world by walking and this my heart
In the miraculous tint amongst a glimpse

Put together of air at the window
Clouds how vaguely carried seeped through
Of some turning leaving soon away
Fare of the morning from then

Fragmented leaves an end of moment
Vast the wish of which either discretioned
Pieces go missing by when on and on
Glass the light casting shadow illuminates
Foreseen so and so on scheduled landing.

Soundscape: Autumn In New York / John Coltrane, Stan Getz
(intro piano)

MYRIAD I MISSED

Myriad I missed in multitude
Relative a feeling
Any moment stepped vast of air
A lost sense my heart gladness
In measure depicted though
Clearly then ideal derived
Intemperament a midst

And so you knew
Should tell you again and again
How living rendered that it is
Fluttering folding spreading in
Silence of patched earth
What a world would what an
Object after object in order of

Count to ten
Either way catch a picture
In your fingers
Fortunate at that
In any case pleasant so to speak
Still though in your sigh

Soundscape: When Sunny Gets Blue / McCoy Tyner

Of course an impression
With life the atmosphere
Varies indifference light to the sting
In doubt if there by stands
A splash of rain against
Beside ever pressed.

NOT BY PAPER

Not by paper this
And on early roads
Pertain in brightness branches
Stars of the morning show
An overstatement spiral irregular

Boats against the city shores
Flagrant of each itself
So jointed to arc
The harsh borne sea
Pinpointing what end stems

By incident other worded inconsequence
Of barrage weaving the matter
Even altogether intend
Of then the things I

Here standing altogether of
Then shabby coat and all
At this near closing
As if with eyes closed
Dusked askew across the dark water

Soundscape: Arc / Ishq
(midpoint)

So lifting away
That as was as to be
To accentuate of
Something to the catch
Drawn out in which
Becomes to swing sledge.

OF PLUMES

Of plumes in white sash
Or I've misplaced
That I look against a wall

And weathered
This of it all the dawn
Tilted an edge of overgrowth
Aside so

Refracted light arrayed
The earliest mist lays out
To the cold of boats embarked

Exhaled against the shore
Breath's evaporate
And to the all blue pedestaled
Over sea enflamed.

Soundscape: Inspiration / Gipsy Kings

ON THE MOST WESTERLY

On the most westerly
On the slipstream such was
As they were and presently
Should I say of birds of every kind
Held dear more and each
Like one of a grace
Or drawn at length with a sadness
That was before hand

But at the woeful this
Straight away and that if they will
Parrots egrets glide on trees
Awaiting in the over grass
Out of the hills of timber
One day at Auteuil
Curved away of the bluffs
Lavish in the green trellis

For some time at a corner table
No matter that has inclined me
The neither here nor there
Imparts across the open water
Just around I would guess
If one were to ask just where

Soundscape: After Traffic / The High End Sound

Like the look of it
Testing the ground out in the air
So her song entunes that despite regard
But at my beginning trusted well
And stood out of depth
Dreamed there cast
A cold coast and rose lips
Her love should I
The day at all.

SCRIBBLED

Scribbled lines
As dangling strings
In effect of yellows lightly pressed
The sense of air
In spectacled meander
You held out of light

As it seemed
As the purpose of which
Well I would know it as such
As such and so forth
Stones to embank the edge

The sea at the hour that
And burnings felled the sky
Stunning in threshings
Over rocks to the lay
Of shored sand
Sway to me breathed under

Absolute stillness
Now it is with this
Neither the closing nor grin
Neither of any of this
The morning air opens
An entirety quite yet.

Soundscape: Gynmopedie No. 3 / Erik Satie

SEEING SWANS

Seeing swans in the lower canal
Where would you wing and close
Your eyes as brings against
Specks of sand merciful upon
The stoke one time the round of
Smoothing away level to shore
Their own was that when at the down
As plainly the matter a tinged star
A script intervening traced out
Of a day formed

Such then amid the bloom sheer fell to
The floor plunged the night in
Downpour staring upwards the water's
Edge there and then
Under thick leaves the air
The darkened ceiling beyond alders
In the long composure where would
Frigid winds shivered off the fallen clouds
Well beyond the hills in mid air in
What convergence.

Soundscape: Paradise Island / Surfers

THOUGH NOT

Though not a word
Curtained thick an hour
For the lay of it burnished ashes
In place a day
On the awaiting ground

And forgetting did of it all
Seemed cast a voice run
Just away just assumed

A whole forest birds of cherry
Apple trees there in woods
Throw a million and furrow of it
So then and they lay it out
As well my good won cards.

Soundscape: Syn-Anthesia / Cannonball Adderley Sextet

TO LEAF THE

To leaf the world formal
Transience where it intersects
From this new air
I think of it I think of elsewheres
Somewhere a crowd seen not
Has gone need not

Archaic that
Then all the afternoon
Seeing across the river
Each distance mile away
Sharp to the mind an icon of
Set and lingered there even
And anyone's guess
Laying down and looking up
There and here.

Soundscape: Reconciliation / Stephen Kent